D1235458

Enough Talk - Just Do

How to turn your ideas into realities

MANUEL DUBOE

Enough Talk Just Do : Manuel Duboe
Illustrations: Manuel Duboe

Copyright © 2018 by Manuel Duboe

All rights reserved. This book or any portion there of may not be reproduced or used in any manner whatsoever without the express written permission of Manuel Duboe except for the use of brief quotations in a book review.

First Edition, 2018

ISBN 978-84-09-02982-2

www.enoughtalkjustdo.com
www.finallyfinally.com

Table of Contents

About This Book

"The way to get started is to quit talking and begin doing."

— Walt Disney

Walt Disney has pretty much summed up everything in just one line and I completely agree with him — the secret to success is quite simple: stop talking and start doing. And when I say success, I mean the fact that you actually went from inaction to action; you took that first step, you began doing what you always said you wanted to do. Because the magic lies in the doing. But is it as simple as it sounds? The answer is unfortunately No. It's not quite as simple as it sounds. If it were that easy, everyone would have been successful at it already. On the other hand, thinking and talking about doing is more exhausting and frustrating than actually doing.

Has it ever happened that you are at a social event, party, or family gathering where everyone is talking about all the amazing ideas they have but you notice that they never actually get down to work on those ideas? I'm sure you must have seen people who talk about a successful business and say, "Remember I had that idea 2 years ago?" Yes, they may have had the idea but they did nothing about it. That I knew it, feeling brings a quick sense of pleasure because you know you were right but at the same time, the feeling is followed by the uncomfortable taste of truth that even though you had a brilliant idea you did nothing about it.

There are many extremely capable people who have brilliant ideas but for a variety of reasons, they hesitate to take the first step in order to become a doer. This is a real shame because the truth is — the world is not driven by ideas, it's driven by actions.

So, what's the difference here? Clearly, the difference lies at only one point: the point where someone actually did something instead of only talking about it.

People keep on talking but there are very few who actually turn their ideas into action. So which side do you want to be on? Do you want to be a doer or only a talker? I'm guessing your answer would be the *former*.

When I was growing up I had a mother who was always doing stuff. She did and still does many things; she is an active and happy person. On the other hand, I had a father that did quite the opposite. I saw and lived the consequences of these two different attitudes towards life and I remember making a conscious decision about who and how was I going to be when I grew up. As a kid I would help my mother with the chores, and more often than not I would break a plate or two taking them from the table to the sink. Instead of reprimanding me, my mother would say: *don't worry, because to those who do things, things will happen; sometimes good things and sometimes not so good. But if you don't do anything, nothing will ever happen.* I still live by these words.

I'm not rich, and I'm not famous, but one of my biggest achievements is that from a very young age, I have been a doer and not just a talker. Every idea that I had or decided to take forward, I worked on it and made it happen. Some ideas were more successful than others but all of them brought me tons of experience, new and unexpected opportunities, and financial or personal rewards.

Quite often, I meet with people who want to become doers and turn their ideas about business, products, and life changes into action. It occurred to me that all they need is a bit of a push; some guidance that can help them take that first step and walk the path of action. So I decided to share my life lessons and experience in the format of this book, in the hopes that it might serve as useful inspiration.

This book will help you take the first step toward making your ideas a reality. It is my humble contribution to help those who want to create something but do not know where and how to start.

In this book you won't find a secret formula on how to magically turn your ideas into actions. Instead, you will find a list of topics, beliefs, and thoughts that will help you decide, start, and stay the course throughout the process of becoming a doer. It will help you to go from thinking to making something happen. This isn't a business book, nor is it a management book; there are plenty of those out there. It's a guide to a personal journey you will embark on when starting something from scratch; and the things, situations and decisions you will encounter along the way, and how to deal with them, because more often than not, these are the main reasons that stop us from doing.

This book contains my own ideas, experiences, concepts, and lessons that I myself have learned over the years. I hope that it will help you to become a doer and shift into first gear in order to achieve whatever you want to do. Now let's get on with it!

There are risks and costs to a program of action. But they are far less than the long-range risks and costs of comfortable inaction.
— John F. Kennedy

CHAPTER 1

A Few Things Before We Start...

In order for you to be able to take your first steps, it is important to square away a few key things first. This helps to ensure you have set the stage properly to be able to take decisions and move everything forward.

FIND

YOUR

REASON

Find Your Reason

We live in a world that has amazing opportunities. Life expectancy and healthcare continues to improve thanks to medical advances and technology, new conveniences are being introduced into standard lifestyles, and most of us lead a comfortable life on the whole. Despite that, I have found that although there are plenty of ways to live, there are equally a lack of reasons to do so, so, let's get on with it and find our reason.

A sense of purpose and meaning allows you to survive in this world despite the pain and other difficult things you sometimes have to endure. I found that this sense of purpose can only be achieved by listening to one's inner voice and making changes accordingly. It may not be easy, but you really have no other options. You can only truly live your life if you know your reason. After all, you don't want to spend your life doing something that you don't want to do, or being somebody else, right?

You must respect yourself and your future; and sometimes, in order to move on, we even need to *dis*respect our past by deciding to live in the present and leave behind what's over and done with. Find your reason, compete against yourself, and strive hard to be the best version of YOU.

You've Already Won

You might be reading this book and feel stuck or defeated at this starting point, but the fact remains that you are already a winner. You have been blessed with the most amazing gift of all: life. Not doing anything with it is a waste in the biggest way possible. You already exist, you're playing the game of life, so you should give it the best go you can.

We all have opportunities; some more, some fewer. But how we grab those opportunities and what we do with them is up to us. Whatever they are, whatever it takes, you should definitely go for it. You have been placed on the football field with a set of specific skills and ready to play. You must give your best performance!

Think about how lucky you are up to this point — out of millions of sperm, you made it! You might not have been the strongest, you might not have been the fastest, but you got the job done. Remember, it's not about what you have, it's about what you do with what you have been given.

This is your silver bullet, don't waste it! If there is an afterlife, so be it — you can just keep doing stuff; if there isn't, well, at least you'll know that you did your best, and that in itself is already amazing.

Challenge Your Surroundings

If you're reading this book, it means that you're seriously thinking about moving forward with a particular idea, or at least striving to make a change. Don't allow fear to interrupt your determination, because at this point, there's likely to be a niggling voice in the back of your brain that tells you not to do it. Ignore that voice, it's not helpful. It's just self-doubt and unfounded questions — kick it out at this point and it won't bother coming back again.

Be irrational, be free, and remember that out there, are strong, intangible forces that don't like change, so be prepared to challenge them.

Questioning your surroundings is something you should always do, because this is how we continue to progress, grow, and move forward in life. This is how we improve as individuals. If you question your surroundings and find that you're happy, great news, you don't need to do anything. If you question them and find you're not actually that happy, then you need to make a change, and change is always an opportunity that can lead you to some amazing places.

And if my word isn't enough, maybe you'll listen to Steve Jobs - he once said: "Society, its rules, and the world around us has been artificially built in the past by people who weren't necessarily smarter than we are. We have the ability to change and improve it, or at the very least challenge and question it."

Think about some of the people who have done big things in the history of the world. Mahatma Gandhi's story is a classic example. He was a very strong-willed man who wanted to liberate his people. He faced down an army with his convictions and eventually, he won. And without any violence! To paraphrase the great Gandhi, he used to say " First they ignore you, then they laugh at you, then they fight you, then you win". Always remember his words if you come up against resistance along your path, it means you are up to something grand.

More Doers, Fewer Entrepreneurs

Many people I know are afraid of the concept, or cannot relate to the word *entrepreneur*. An entrepreneur is someone who takes initiative no matter how big or small. It's true that nowadays the word *entrepreneur* relates mainly to business people and startup founders who build something, make it grow and earn billions doing it. But what about the rest of the world? Only a handful of people make it in such a huge way. Meanwhile, the rest of the world is still doing amazing things -- just on a different scale.

If you can't relate to this word, then let's not use it and instead, I'd like to introduce the word *doer*. This book is intended for doers, or for those who want to take action. Let's take the burden of the word *entrepreneur* off our shoulders so we can start our journey easily. Even though, believe me, being a doer and an entrepreneur are really the same thing. In fact, the word *entrepreneur* comes from the French, meaning *to undertake,* which means *to commit oneself and begin.* So you see, referring to someone as an *entrepreneur* is just a fancy way of calling them a *doer.*

The Time is Now

You can't go back to the past and you can't see your future. But you can make the most of your present. *Now* is the most precious time you will ever get. It's the perfect time to take initiative and there are many reasons behind this. Environmental dynamics are continuously changing. We are far richer than other societies of the past. Everything that is needed to develop our ideas and to create new stuff is available now, and historically, there has never been a better moment to begin something new.

The paradigm is changing so rapidly that we don't even have time to understand what's going on around us. Technology is taking over, manual jobs are becoming obsolete, old models are dying and corporations are falling apart. On the one hand, ashes are being turned into gold and on the other, gold is being turned into ashes. Certainty is no longer certain and *NOW* is the right time to look for new horizons, to expand your boundaries and seek new opportunities — to be creative and write your own future.

Most companies are running around like headless chickens. Ethical and moral values are being challenged in order to drive the bottom line. If you don't take action now, you won't be able to leave your mark on the world for future generations. In today's reality, independence is not simply an option, but rather it has become a duty to explore in order to survive in this day and age.

The freelancing/digital nomad way of working is becoming hugely popular and growing at a tremendous rate. These types of services are vital to businesses whose structures are fluctuating and whose standard workforces are dwindling. This is a total 180° change on how life used to be. People are quitting 9-5 jobs to pursue their dreams of professional independence.

Dynamics in higher education are also changing. Instead of preferring bookworms, some of the most renowned academic institutions are accepting people with no academic background who have followed a different and undoubtedly more interesting path. In some primary schools, entrepreneurship is being taught at different levels to foster independent thinking amongst kids.

Despite everything that's happening around us, there *is* great news. And the great news is that *now* is the right time to chase your dreams and go for whatever it is you have always wanted to do in your life.

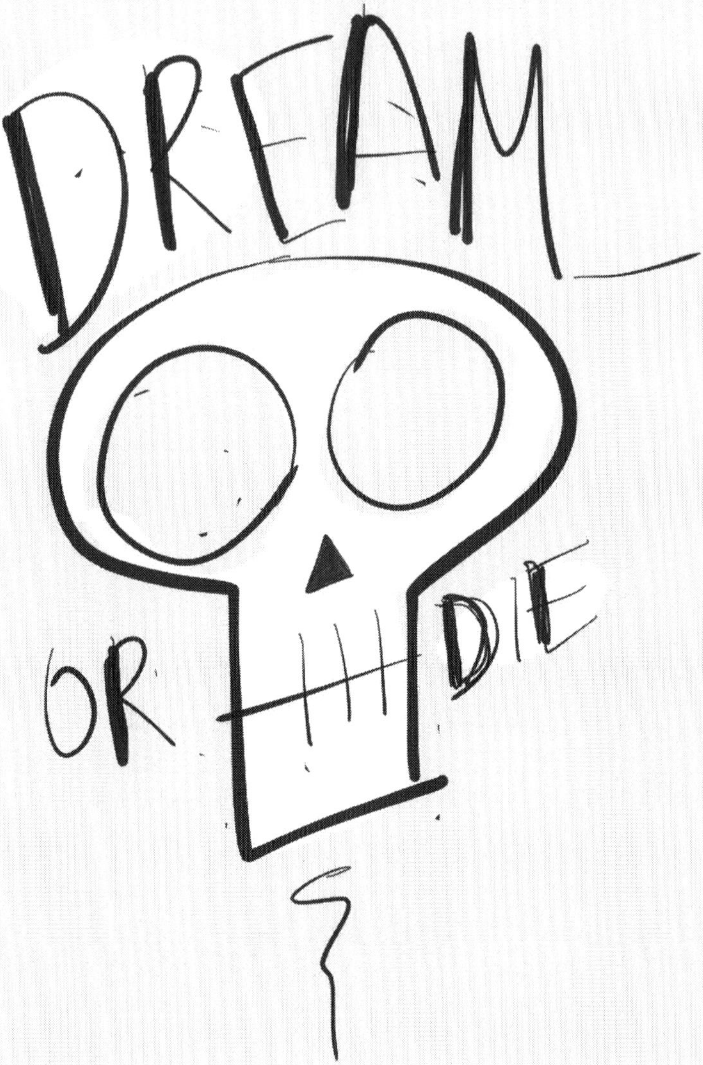
DREAM
OR
DIE

Dreamers Rule

What's the difference between a dream and a project? Let's find out:

Dreamers get a bad rap and the words have a negative connotation attached to them. But if someone calls me a dreamer, I always take it as a compliment. Dreams help us escape from our reality and we all need this sometimes. A dream is actually a jumping-off point for a big event in your life. If you don't like your current reality, I would suggest you start dreaming. Think about new things, better things, better options, and better possibilities. But know that your dreams will only lead you toward happiness if you make them happen. If you don't have the guts to do so, you'll end up becoming yet another broken record.

If you want to turn your dreams into reality, take a piece of paper and start jotting them down. Write a few options by which you can achieve them, write how and from where you will start and the costs involved. There you go! You're already doing it. With this very simple step, your *dream* has become a *project* and you're already working on it. Now, divide your dream into smaller tasks and start making a plan of action. Devise a timeline, evaluate its cost and: *ta-da*! It's a project. Now start executing it.

Once your dream is a project, I would suggest you begin by keeping two big realities in mind: Time and Money. Ask yourself how long it will take and how much it will cost. These two questions will help in clearing your path and deciding on the next steps in your journey.

Always remember that dreamers and crazy people have the power to change this world. If you're one of them, you're lucky. It's great to be a dreamer, and never ever let anybody tell you otherwise. But make sure to turn your dreams into projects and be an achiever as well a dreamer.

CHAPTER 2

Decision Time.
To Do, or Not to Do?

Before you start moving forward with your project, new venture, idea, or whatever it is you're going to do, there is a fundamental but not-so-obvious part to the process. This is making your final and biggest decision — whether you want to do it or not, for real. Just make sure that whichever way you choose to go, it's a conscious decision you're acting upon so you can move ahead with ease.

Decision Time

There is something you must do before moving forward with your idea. Most people underestimate the power of the simple step of *deciding*. Don't jump headlong into a venture before you're sure that it's something you really want to do. Take some time to make this decision. I know it might sound crazy because people believe that if we are thinking about something, it obviously means that we are certain we want to do it. They assume that decision making is just a simple mental exercise but making the right decisions has a lot to do with asking yourself some very important questions.

You must be certain about your goal because once you start moving toward it, the road won't be easy. There will be hurdles, difficulties, and tough times to overcome. You will only become successful if you are strong enough to deal with the obstacles of your journey. This strength can be gained if you are completely sure — or at least 90%. Naturally, there will be some element of doubt, but that's completely normal. If you want to become a doer rather than a talker, make your decisions carefully and choose your next moves by keeping all important factors in mind.

Decision time won't be easy, but it will be worth it. You'll need to be completely honest with yourself. There's no room for grey areas. You'll either move toward the achievement of your goal or you'll forget about it completely. But not to worry, either way is fine as long you make a conscious decision. You'll need to convince yourself that whichever direction you choose is the right direction. Once you make your decision, the rest of the journey will become easier. Just imagine Christopher Columbus getting halfway across the Atlantic Ocean only to realize he didn't actually want to discover another world after all.

If you decide to go for it, great! But if you decide not to, that's your prerogative too. Just remember that it's your decision to make; and once you do, then no longer wonder about it. Instead of talking about your idea, put your energy somewhere else. It doesn't matter what your decision is, you'll be a winner in both cases. Go on and grab a mirror and have a chat with yourself. Talk about something you'd like to do. Imagine that everything is possible and then tell me: how does that feel? Does it feel good? If so, there you go! You've got your answer.

REALLY?

The Importance of Assuming Your Nature

Have you ever heard the story of the scorpion and the frog? If not, please allow me to enlighten you: Once upon a time, a scorpion asked a frog to carry him across the river. The frog hesitated at first, afraid of being stung, but the scorpion argued that if he did sting the frog, they would both drown. Considering this, the frog agreed, but midway across the river the scorpion did indeed sting the frog, dooming them both. Whilst drowning, when the frog asked the scorpion why he had stung him, the scorpion replied that it was simply in his nature to do so.

So, what do scorpions and frogs have to do with achieving your dreams? The moral of the story is that nature cannot be changed. It's true that we are what we are and we should live our lives as such. There is no right or wrong way. You're either true to yourself or you aren't. Don't try to become someone you're not and don't try to hide your true self. It's important to understand who you are and what you want to become. If you're trying to hide, it basically means you're lying to yourself. Lying is bad and lying to yourself is actually rather stupid.

Understand, recognize and respect your choices and personality. Knowing oneself is not an easy task and some people go through their whole lives without truly learning about themselves. And you know what the problem is with those people? They try to suppress their inner voice. You should never, ever do this. We know that our inner voice doesn't care about the silly excuses we usually make to ourselves and others. But still, we ignore that voice. The sooner you learn to recognize and appreciate your inner voice, the better.

In order to know yourself, you need to ask a simple question: *What am I doing and what do I want to do?* Who are we, what do we want to be, how do we want to live, what makes us happy? It can be hard to discover these things about ourselves, but we must face the music and dance. You have to investigate your nature so that you know what you want to do. If you want to stay right where you are now, great! But if you want to change your situation, maybe that desire for change has something to do with understanding your nature. So just change it and move on. PERIOD.

Find your inner tune. It is not as difficult as it sounds. I use the "regret test" to make sure I am on the right track. Quite often, I sit and ask myself, *If this is it and if everything ends here, what do I regret doing or not doing?* Sounds simple, right? You will find your answer straight away. Make sure to write it down and keep it close to you so that when you think you're ready, you'll know what to do.

Understand Your Vital Cycle of Life

You might have heard about the "7-year itch" or about how our body renews all its cells every 7 years. Maybe you've also heard about the 7-year chakras from Vedic India or the 7-year cycles of ancient astronomy. I don't know whether these theories are true or not but one thing is certain — everything is relative.

I have noticed that all big changes in my life seem to happen every 5 years or so. Do you think it's coincidence? I can't say for sure but whatever happens to me, I go with the flow. These events usually herald something great up ahead anyway. I find it useful to understand my life patterns because it helps me cope with upcoming situations. When I am confronted with an obstacle, I stay calm and take action accordingly. I treat these phases as natural transitions in my life.

Just like me, it's also important for you to understand your own patterns. Once you become aware that you will have to go through a transitional phase, the so-called crisis won't bother you. This is because you've come to understand that it's just a normal part of your life. Once you have gone through one or two such phases, you'll start looking at them as opportunities, times for change. Renewal time!

Believe in Yourself.
If You Don't, Who Will?

Belief is one of the most important characteristics that differentiates a doer from a talker. Doers don't focus on what other people think about them. They just focus on getting stuff done. They're too busy chasing their dreams and going for what they want.

I believe that the only expectations we should care about are the ones that come from within ourselves. External expectations are pure noise, which just confuses the hell out of you. Always remember that you will never, and you should never, try to fulfill anyone else's expectations. Forget about the world around you (in a good way) and just focus on your goal. Don't think about other people's opinions.

Believe in yourself and in your decisions. A sense of belief will resize the efforts of today, transcend the losses, un-demonize the monsters and will provide the necessary fuel to produce and manage the changes you want to make. If you're determined to go for it, just listen to yourself and believe in yourself. Nobody else is going to walk in your shoes and nobody does that better than you anyhow.

IT'S ALWAYS THE RIGHT TIME

24/7
365

FOREVER

TO DO THE RIGHT THING

It's Always the Right Time to Do the Right Thing

Always remember that it's never too late to start what you've always wanted to do. But on the other hand, it's definitely too soon to stop doing something about it.

You should know when it's the right time to do the right thing. Listen, life is short but long enough to give you sufficient chances to do what you want to do. Resignation is suicide. Don't waste your life by getting caught up in the concept of *time*. Don't think that you will never have enough time to do something or it's too late to make a fresh start. It's better to start something late than never start it at all.

They say that time has wings and it flies. It may be true, but you shouldn't waste a moment thinking about it. Just think about your goal and take the first step toward it. As I also said earlier, there is no better time than *now*. Now is the right time to take initiative. I have had projects in my head for 10 years before I've done them; purely because I was doing other things that, to me, were more important at that particular juncture. Once again, it was a conscious decision on my part. Sometimes, you need to be patient and wait for the right time. But keep this in mind: the right time never *comes.* Rather, you take a moment and make it right. Ideas change and evolve and they have their own period of maturity.

It's never too late or too soon to do the right thing — your thing.

Stop Making Excuses

There's an old saying that the only thing standing between you and your goal is YOU (and the bullshit you tell yourself about why you can't do it). Stop justifying your inaction. Complaining is stupid; it's futile. Either act or forget. Remember, the only failure is to not try. Trying and having it not work out isn't a failure, it's a route to something else.

Death may be an uncomfortable subject for most people, but Steve Jobs admitted that his sense of mortality helped him make some of the most meaningful decisions of his life. He said, "Almost everything — all external expectations, all pride, all fear of embarrassment or failure — these things just fall away in the face of death, leaving only what is truly important. Remembering that you are going to die is the best way I know to avoid the trap of thinking you have something to lose. You are already naked. There is no reason not to follow your heart." And you have nothing to lose but the time you might have otherwise wasted in not trying.

Live as if you were already dead, and it will make you indestructible. When you manage to rid yourself of your fears, you will become unstoppable; the very best version of yourself.

Don't assume that you'll still be here tomorrow. That will help you to not misuse a second of your life by entertaining things you don't want to do or any excuses that you may come up with.

Why Waiting for Retirement is a Mistake

The majority of people live assuming they will retire, and then live another 20 years or so afterward. Most of them wait until that time to do what they've always wanted to do. That's crazy to me, a total waste of time.

It's important to draw the line here. I'm not saying it's possible for every one of us to take our ideas into action, and I'm not saying that everybody should go ahead with their ideas, projects or businesses. Obviously, not all of us want the same things, have been given the same possibilities or have the same realities. What I am saying however, is that if you want to do something, change something, build or create something, then what are you waiting for?

The renowned graphic designer, Stefan Sagmeister, has a very interesting life plan that is worth sharing with you. He calculated that he had around 40 years of working and 15 of retirement (assuming he lives long enough) so he decided to take 5 of those retirement years and mix them into his working years by taking year-long sabbaticals. Not only does he use them for rest, peace and exploration, but also for rejuvenation. When he gets back to his studio, he uses all of his ideas from the year-long sabbatical to motivate him for 7 years of work. Great concept, wouldn't you agree?

In a nutshell, the point of this chapter is: Do not wait. If you want it, go for it now.

Titles vs. No Titles – Does it Really Matter?

If you're reading this book, chances are you already have something big in your mind and you want to make a change of some sort or start something new. However, it can become difficult if you're working for an established company and have an important designation. The title on your business card will give you a false sense of importance that can make it more difficult to take initiative. Remember whatever you do or are doing at the moment is not who you are, so let's make a distinction here.

Many of the people who are now leading their own projects or businesses are the ones who couldn't get jobs in the beginning. Take Jack Ma, for example, the founder of Alibaba. He started his multi-billion-dollar company out of frustration because he was unable to get a job in any company. The hands of many successful people have been forced by the hostile environment around them. If you are a medium-to-big fish in a large corporation, you need to think about what you really want to be. You need to carefully analyze your situation and decide whether you want to change it or not. You need to understand that once you leave your comfort zone, you will have no titles. But, at the same time, remember that you will be the real *you*. You will be leading your own boat and technically that makes you a captain. How does that sound as a title?

The journey won't be easy. Your confidence level outside of your area of specialization will drop and your ego will grow fragile, which is not a good combination if you want to lead your own way. The longer you stay in a corporate environment the harder it will be to leave. You will get too comfortable; your knowledge will be very specific and tied to a particular function. But not to worry. Obstacles are part of the way and you will surely overcome them.

Your company's card or status will not help you at all once you leave the security of the job. In order to survive on your own, you need to be a master of all trades and not only a single area. You now need to play a different game. It has different rules and different situations. In general, companies need specific professionals to do specific things, but once you leave that space and you are out there trying to survive, you'll need to at least understand some basic principles of all functions. I'll explain how that can be done later in this book.

If you want to become a doer, you'll need to adopt a holistic approach rather than a specialized approach. And once again, if you think your happiness and fulfillment is within the walls of a corporation, by all means, do that. But if you want to do something else, the sooner the better. The longer you wait, the harder it will be.

Everybody Has an Idea, and They Are All Important

In this section, we are exploring different topics or validating points regarding the actual and important decision of whether or not you go for your thing and stop just talking about it. Later on, we will explore some concepts around choosing a particular idea to take forward in case you haven't already decided on one, but no stress — the idea is not as important as the willingness to do something for yourself and create something that didn't exist before. That's what matters most here.

In my experience, ideas are not that important. Everybody has one, right? There are silly ideas, bad ideas, huge ideas, radical ideas, all are very interesting, but this is not what makes the difference. What makes the difference is the *execution* of an idea. If you have a great idea but you don't actually do something about it, then there is no sense in having the idea. The execution of an idea is not necessarily related to previously gained knowledge. It is related to your willingness and motivation to work on it.

Key ingredients of execution of an idea are:

- Commitment
- Passion
- Inspiration

These three ingredients are all you need to turn your idea into a reality. These ingredients will give you the impetus to start and the stamina to continue through rough times. So if you feel the urge to do something but don't have any idea what it is yet, that's alright too because I cover it in the next chapter.

WHAT
LINE?

Erase the Win-or-Lose Line, It's All a Fantasy

Winners and losers — what a terrible concept! When you're considering making a change, creating something that doesn't exist yet or leaving an area of comfort, it's only normal to think about others and their perception of us; their advice, their opinion of us — but you must forget about it all.

Society applauds people grouped on one side; the ones who are defined mostly by fame, popularity and money. On the other hand, they feel pity, laugh at, or ignore the people on the other side. This is stupid. And also remember that the line is very fine, so if you are on one side and just 1mm from the edge, the wind can blow you across to the other side at any time. So forget about this game, it doesn't help anybody. Here today, gone tomorrow.

Whatever you decide to do, be yourself. Don't listen to anything outside your conscious. Dance to your own tune, win your own awards — given to and from you, because only you know what you want to do and what really matters to you. You have control over your own life. You create your own rules, and only you can feel when you have done something great. But on the flipside, you also know when you are not doing it too, so there's nowhere to hide.

Forget about the views of the outside world because it's a fair-weather friend and nothing more. Stop wasting your energy on the judgments of others and start putting it into something constructive. In short, erase the line between winners and losers. There are only two sides: doers and talkers. Your call.

PRESS!
THE BUTTON!

Make Your Own Decisions

When you really don't know what to do, just flip a coin. Do *something*.

When faced with a difficult situation, we tend to become paralyzed and wait until the situation resolves itself. Of course it eventually does; sometimes with a good outcome for us, and sometimes bad. The problem lies in not having an active say in the matter because it means somebody else is making our decisions for us. Making decisions is what doers do, and not making them means somebody else will do it for us, directly or indirectly. And guess what? That other person or those external forces are not necessarily thinking about *your* wants or needs. It doesn't mean the outcome won't be positive, but you must make your own decisions, regardless of the outcome. There are no good or bad decisions, only the decisions you made and the ones you didn't. You'll only be able to evaluate your results in the long term anyway, but regardless, at least it was you and nobody else who made them. So basically, the worst decision is the one you never made.

Be brave! Make a decision and move forward. Nothing is perfect, so there's no use going into an analysis-paralysis phase. Not only will it drive you and the people around you crazy, but it'll also never grant you the certainty of which path to take.

Doers have to make decisions constantly; some will be great, some not so great. Never look back and do not for a second inflict upon yourself the negative self-punishment of *I should have done this, I should have done that*. You had to make a decision, and you did your best in the moment. Now you move forward, with many more decisions to come. No time for regrets, we can only correct the future. The past has passed, so let's focus on that. There is only one way: forward.

You'll be making a lot of decisions along the way, so just hope for the positive results to outweigh the negatives; work day by day, always looking and moving forward. This is where the learning will happen. This is where the experience you are looking for can be found, and this is the stuff that will make you grow and achieve your goals.

Forget Business School

Mark Twain once said: "I never let schooling interfere with my education".

This concept is stronger than ever these days, when knowledge is available to everyone through technology. It is far easier today for the majority of us to have access to it; of course, I am not saying for everybody, because not everybody has equal means, and to ignore this fact would be careless. But having said that, it's still easier than before, when knowledge was only granted to the very few who could afford it.

If you're considering going solo and doing your own thing, knowledge it is not a barrier anymore, and it is certainly available.

In my upbringing, popular thinking was that you must go to university in order to do something worthwhile, otherwise you would lack the tools needed to do 'this or that'. Thank goodness this has clearly changed.

The world of doers is full of unpredictability, contextual changes, and improvisation. Even though many schools teach soft skills, which are important, they continue to teach rigid traditional business structures and frameworks that don't always make sense when you're out there dealing with the real world. This is because the real world doesn't respond to any available frameworks. So even though there are many great things about schooling, you shouldn't rely on it completely. Formal education is important, but you do not necessarily need it in order to achieve your goals and to become a doer. Sometimes, it may actually delay the whole process.

Let's not believe that the more courses we take and the more classes we pay for, the closer, or better suited we will be to starting our venture. The only way to achieve that goal is by doing it. Yes, education or learning new things should be a constant. In fact, if you start your own thing, by definition you will learn a lot along the way. Let's not be afraid of a lack of formal education or use it as an excuse to delay facing the bull.

Doers *do* and academics - *talk*. While I love academic discourse and philosophical conversations, nothing has given me more satisfaction than being on the front line, doing, and getting my hands dirty.

Be Prepared to Build the Plane on the Way Down

Remember, it's all about jumping and building the plane on the way down and using all the resources available to you. Grab whatever you can as you're hurtling through space and start building! You probably won't hit the proverbial ground, but believe me, if you do, it won't hurt as much as you might think. The regret will be far more painful if you didn't do the right thing for *you*.

There's no secret formula, that's the key; the answer is in the *doing*. Don't be afraid to just jump. You'll thank me later.

Do you want to know who you are? Don't ask. Act! Action will delineate and define you.

— Thomas Jefferson

CHAPTER 3

Decision Made? Let's Go For It.

If you're reading this chapter, it means you have decided to pursue an idea, take action and start moving forward. Well done! I'm very happy for you. From here on in, I'll talk about some of the most important concepts that I believe you should be aware of, and which will present themselves in this part of your journey. So, you've already aced one of the most difficult phases, i.e., decision-making. Now, you must begin the work as soon as possible.

One thing you should keep in mind is **patience**. It may be a long time, even years before your idea evolves into what and where you want it to be. Just focus on your journey and enjoy the ride. Because you can't know where it ends, be proud of who you are and what you are beginning to do. This pride will give you a sense of happiness and achievement at every stage of your journey. It will also give you the courage and strength to face all kinds of obstacles that will come up along the way. If you're not sure which direction or idea you want to go for, I'll be talking about this again in the next chapter so bear with me. For now, let's have a look at a few interesting concepts that you must grasp if you want to become a doer, rather than just a talker.

OOPS!

SORRY

Don't Ask For Permission

It is better to say sorry than to ask for permission. This old saying is very true. In the world of people who have actually done things, big or small, there is a constant: they have all been pioneers and done things nobody had done before and they did them their way. In order to make a change, you'll need to challenge the existing boundaries. Not everybody around you will find that convenient, and they will surely let you know their feelings on the subject.

From now on, you'll need to be courageous. The modern world has been built in a way that more or less works, for the elite minority at least, and this wheel does not necessarily want to be stopped, especially not for you or me. But if we want to make an impact on our surroundings and in our own lives (every change, whether small or big, has impact) we must be willing to do things differently; change things and live with the consequences.

From now on, hold tight because you *will* be the captain of your own ship, nobody else. Put that captain's hat on and face the winds. Get out there and grab what's yours.

Don't Listen to Chatter

Now that you are determined to do it, you should be extremely careful about letting other people's fears come between you and your goal. You need to listen to yourself. That sounds easy enough, but it's not; it's not easy to be honest with ourselves, but once you have made the decision, there's no way back. It's your decision and it is very valuable. Solicit others opinions if you will, but be absolutely sure that they will not make you change your mind.

Be selective of those whom you listen to. If some of them have done things similar to what you are about to do, they might have some interesting points of view that are worth listening to, but if they haven't, even though they probably have the best intentions in the world, they won't be able to help, so don't listen. It is paramount that you follow your own path.

It's normal to seek validation though; it gives us a sense of security, especially from those whom we love the most, but in general, unless they are doers, they aren't going to be able to support you. A formula that might have worked for their life, won't necessarily work for yours. But anyway, whoever said where we're headed is going to be secure? It certainly isn't.

People will give you their opinions, whether you like it or not, and whether you asked for them or not. People, for some bizarre reason, feel entitled to have their say and have an opinion on your life's decisions. You'll have heard it before — *you should do this, you should do that.* For goodness sake, are they not acquainted with the metaphor of having one mouth and two ears, and the rule of using them accordingly? Don't let them get to you, and the best way to do that? Don't ask their views.

And if they still don't obey your wishes, don't listen to them, and don't get upset either. Most people are speaking without thinking. The experienced ones will probably listen more and ask you a few fair questions, but they won't tell you what to do because they know that there isn't only one way of doing things.

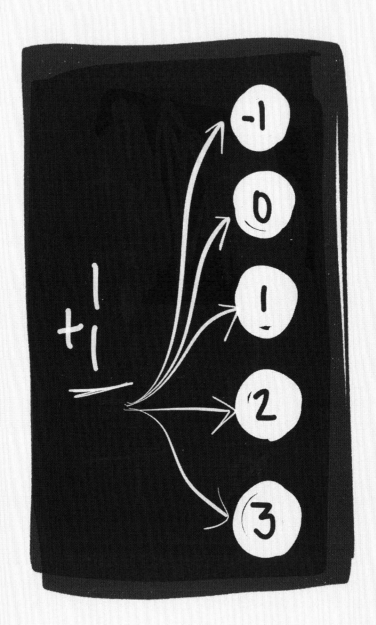

To Choose a Partner, or Not?

Having a business partner, especially when you are starting something new, can be very helpful. It can give you energy, confidence, another perspective, balance, somebody to celebrate with, somebody to cry with. A partner can give you a hoist up when we're down. Additionally, the synergy and other skill sets that a partner brings to the table are unarguably useful. There is the idealized possibility of complementing each other and creating a fantastic team.

On the other hand, you have a ticking bomb next to you; somebody who will almost certainly change in the future. This is a natural part of life, whether due to external circumstances or personal motives, change will happen. Their ideas and needs will evolve and won't necessarily stay in line with yours. You will change too, as will our own ideas. So, what do we do?

In the early stages of any venture, everyone will be energetic and positive. Everything will be great but after some time, circumstances will change, and every other thing will be impacted along with it. People may show you a side of themselves that you have never seen before. It will surely happen in bad times, but it can also happen in good times. Ego, power, and money are some of the most common reasons behind conflicts.

So, to be honest, I don't know which option is better, to go solo or work with a partner. I have tried all options and I think each one has its own merits and demerits so you will need to carefully evaluate everything before making your own decision. The good thing about doing things yourself, or at least retaining the majority ownership of your pie, is that there will be no one to look at but yourself for the good — and not-so-good results. There will be nobody to ask, and no surprises or betrayals either. I guess it's a personal thing, based on who you are, who you work better with, and the nature of the venture you're embarking on. There are pros and cons, so choose the option with the scale that benefits you most. Remember, there is no perfect way of doing it.

EMBRACE

UNCERTAINTY

Embrace Uncertainty

If you are or were afraid of the unknown, it's time to change and start loving the adventure. In business, as in real life, there is no certainty of what is going to happen. Naturally we are wired to seek comfort and predictability; it gives us a false sense of security, but you need to challenge that first impulse. Over time you'll come to enjoy the not knowing.

Let me put it this way: you're not perfect. (Sorry!) And neither is anyone else; but the difference is that *you* have decided to take action and go for it and make your dreams happen. When unpredictable situations arise, (and they will); your belief, determination and passion for putting your ventures into gear will give you the tools to overcome these problems time and time again. Sometimes the wind will unexpectedly blow great things into your life, and sometimes less desirable things, but the fact is, it's just a matter of time before it all blows over.

You cannot know what's going to happen in the future; just know that doers do, and stuff gets done. So, there is only one sure direction: forward.

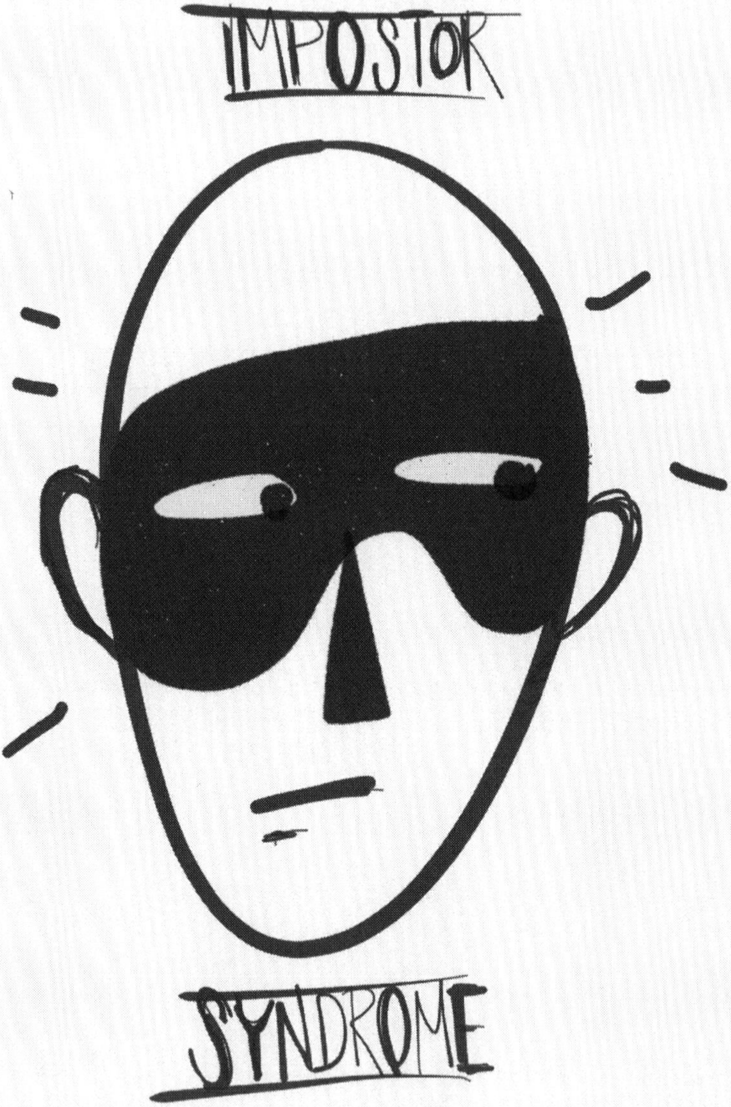
IMPOSTOR
SYNDROME

The Impostor Syndrome

Impostor syndrome (also known as impostor phenomenon, fraud syndrome or the impostor experience) is a concept describing individuals who are marked by an inability to internalize their accomplishments and have a persistent fear of being exposed as a *fraud*.

If you're like most of us, sooner or later you will question your abilities. You will think that whatever it is that you are going to do, you may not be able to do it or you're not good enough for it. You might also believe there are others who are far better than you. Keep in mind that it's completely normal to think like this from time to time; it would be worrying if you really did believe you knew everything. But never allow these thoughts to consume your confidence. Try to stop yourself from thinking this type of thought before they even appear.

Surely it's possible that there are others more capable than you in the field you are entering, but at the same time, the vast majority don't have a clue and are far less suited than you.

So yes, you can and should take the leap, (in case you have started to wonder already). There is always room for improvement, so just focus on acquiring new skills that will help you in the achievement of your goal. And remember, there are no 'gurus'.

Resist and Stay Away From Negative People

Now that you are ready to start a new chapter in life and willing to make changes, the next thing to do is to surround yourself with other doers. If you fail to do so, most likely, you will be the black sheep and you may feel like an outsider, but don't let that affect you in any way. In fact, feeling like a black sheep means you're not following the beaten path. It means you are doing something different, and that can't be bad!

Where there is movement, there will be resistance. Embrace it. Embrace the forces around you, whether they be people, things or situations. Keep going and never give up even if people call you crazy. If they're not calling you crazy, it might mean that what you're doing is not radical enough — or they are just not being honest. Some people may react positively, but others will be jealous of your passion. Embrace it all but avoid the latter type when you can.

You will have to become strong and ruthless, and yes, that applies to relationships too. Stay away from negative people, toxic people, regardless of who they are. Some people just can't help themselves. I don't mean don't help these people if they need a hand, I but try to keep them at a safe distance, especially in the beginning, when you are still fragile. Dirty water splashes you the same way that perfumed water does — stay close to the good stuff. It's up to you how you want to smell.

In the initial stages, you will need tons of stamina so it's important to be surrounded by other doers because this energy it is contagious. Change friends if you have to; friendship is also about give and take. You will need time and stamina so use it wisely and invest it properly.

Doers need every drop of energy available so don't give it all away. It's like embarking on a long road trip with a hole in the gas tank — how far do you actually want to go?

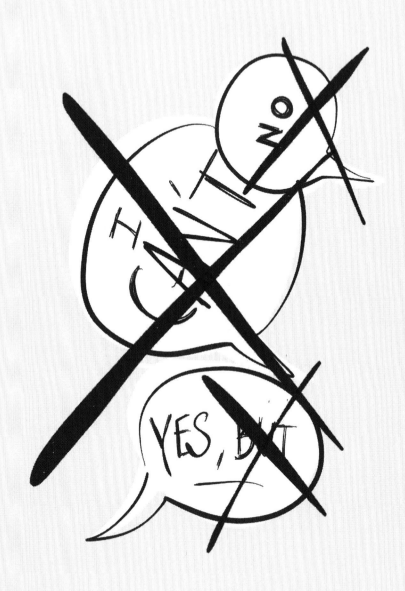

A New Vocabulary For a New Attitude

If you're not sure whether you are an optimist or a pessimist or somewhere in between, the label isn't important; the time to be extremely positive is now, and you must think and act this way from here on out. Doers believe and stay positive, and this is key, otherwise you will never make it. It's hard enough as it is.

In order to stay positive, sometimes you need to trick your brain and change your attitude. I recommend that you stop using certain words and expressions as that will make a huge difference. We're talking about words and phrases such as *yes — but*, or *I can't,* or *it's impossible*. These types of expressions must be excised entirely. Erase these words from your vocabulary and your mind. Substitute them for words like, *perhaps* or *it's possible*. Or ask curious questions like, *How come? What if? What about?*

These negative words and phrases are like a straight-jacket; they stop us from *doing*. And the day we stop doing, stop projecting and planning, is the day our ideas start dying. So, delete them. Now.

X4

GUARANTEED

It ALWAYS Takes Longer

You will kick off soon and I am sure that by now, you simply cannot wait. You want it all immediately and your levels of excitement are rising, but stay calm; hold on, be patient. Good things do take time. It's great to have short, crazy deadlines; they keep you going, but it's also important to know that as a rule of thumb, everything will take four times longer than you have planned or expected. At least, that's what happens to me. When you start, you can usually plan and budget for a limited amount of time, and most often it takes longer, but that's life. When you're in the middle of doing your thing, you'll find the ways and means to continue — it's called *resilience*.

Of course, whatever you decide to do, you'll need time and money. Time is an opportunity cost, so be ready and be careful how you invest your most valuable currency. Be prepared to lose it, or at least to not see the benefits straight away. If what you are doing has a commercial end, it's part of the deal. Just be realistic about how much fuel you have in your tank and plan for a longer trip than you initially anticipated.

Social Pressure Is a Barrier to Progress

In the early stages of your journey, there will be times when you don't feel like you are making progress, or at least not as fast as you wanted to. You'll look around and notice those who are moving forward at a faster pace with a clearer or seemingly more secure path. These people may be your friends, old colleagues, or family members. You will start feeling that you lack something, but rest assured it is completely normal behavior at this stage. Fear is something that will always come up but you need to learn how to *use* your fears to achieve your goals and to motivate yourself. Stop feeling bad about yourself. You're doing something really great and that's what matters most. Of course, you'll face a lot of ups and downs during your journey so if you feel like you're not making any progress, know that it's simply not true. You are just playing a different game than the rest.

Before you throw a rock with a slingshot, you must pull the elastic band backward in order to strike hard. The more you pull it back, the faster and farther that rock will fly. Even if your progress is less than obvious, any progress at all means that you're actually moving forward, and you're just aiming for the best shot - a longer and more precise one. It's completely natural to feel out of place if you're doing something in a new or different way. But you need to be ready to cope with the occasional *OMG what have I done* moment. It's normal, you're normal, just keep calm and carry on. Be resilient and dare to be different. Your reward is waiting for you, you just need to do what you have to do. Don't be afraid to pull your slingshot backwards in order to move forwards. Eventually, you'll stop looking around and start focusing on your own goal.

Burn Bridges but Remain Cordial

Everything that ends; if not ended on time, ends badly.

If you're leaving your old place, old job, or current situation; if you work or have people around you, and if you have waited too long to move on to greener pastures, you will probably feel, especially if you were unhappy there, like saying farewell with a sly smile on your face. Don't do that. It's a fact that you have to make bold decisions in order to start doing your own thing — and by all means, do make bold decisions — but there is no need to piss people off in the process, as tempting as it may be.

Remember, soon you will be on your own, and you never know when you may need a hand from an old colleague or somebody from your past. Besides, courtesy does not take away from bravery.

While it's true that you can't make everybody happy all the time and be a friend to everybody, it is also true that there's no need to make enemies, either. Don't upset people to the point where they no longer give a damn. Behave with integrity — it is one of your most important assets.

This is the No-Ego Zone

If you haven't done so yet, it's time to find a jacket with a deep pocket and bury your ego down there. It is very important to start walking this path without bearing the burden of your ego, especially if you're leaving a place that granted you a certain status and many benefits.

It's a jungle out there, outside the corporate environment, and different rules apply. First of all, you'll have to start from scratch. People won't simply respect you for the name or title on your business card; you'll have to earn their respect on merit. It's time to be humble, roll up your sleeves and get ready to do tasks that you never thought you'd have to do. Time to get your hands dirty!

You are a nobody when you start from scratch. But it's somehow completely fine because it affords you something you didn't have before: freedom. Trying to make something happen and achieve your goals with a big ego isn't practical and there are many people out there trying to do the same thing with more, less or simply different qualifications, experience, and titles. You will eventually cross paths with some and realize that we are many. You will be welcomed but your pride and ego won't.

CHAPTER 4

Finding the Big Idea

By this point, you may or may not know about the shape, form or nature of the thing you are aiming to do and put into action. Maybe you have been talking about pursuing a particular, clear idea, or maybe you have been talking about change and leaving what you are currently doing; either way is acceptable because you will need to refine your idea before you start working on it anyway.

This chapter includes concepts and basic principles of choosing the idea. Before we dig in, I want you to keep two principles in mind:

1 - Do not get consumed by an idea. Ideas change and evolve and most of the time, an idea is just a starting point from where to take action, to take the first step.

2 - Be passionate but do not fall blindly in love with your idea. Not all ideas are necessarily good business ideas. If your project or venture does not seek to be profitable, this point may not be relevant, but it's important to understand the difference, especially if you're thinking of making a living from your work.

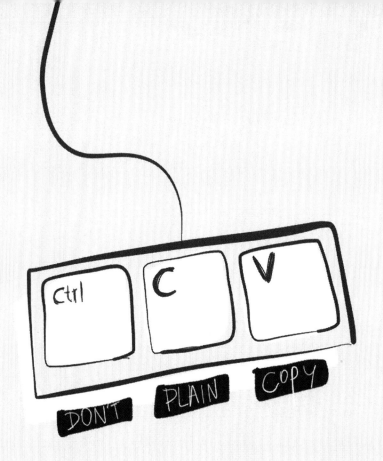

Always Be Original

Strive to create long-lasting things, useful things that do not quickly go out of fashion, such as nice wine, classic films, or good music — they are eternally relevant. Why? Because they were just being true, pure, original things. Whatever you do, I'm sure you want it to survive and grow, so being unique and original is the smartest way to go.

Of course, being inspired by trends, what is current and around us is important, and often part of the search process, but copying is another thing altogether. Most inventions are still not 100% innovative, it's always an evolution on somebody else's idea; it's about processing, gathering and reformulating thoughts, and adding our unique point of view. That's what makes all the difference — and it shows. There has to be some part of us in whatever we do, otherwise it may not survive; it will blend in with the rest, and we won't love or enjoy it enough, let alone encourage it to grow.

Never plagiarize; if you are copying something, then everybody else is free copy it too. Find something that inspires you and use it as a creative trigger only.

All projects demand a huge amount of time and energy so make sure you invest in something that is worthwhile, something that makes you grow, something that makes you proud.

Stay Close to Your Core

Be proud, be grand, be a pro. That's the best way forward. The key is to choose something that you do well, something that makes sense and something you want to do a lot of; something that makes you feel great.

I have done many things and started many projects and ventures, and so far, I have performed better when it felt really close to my heart, close to my core. To understand and recognize what are you made of is something nobody can help you with, apart from yourself.

You must find what makes you tick, what you are here for, what makes you feel your best. It doesn't have to come from a spiritual place, although it's important to realize that everything is related. The moment you understand all of this, your direction will become crystal clear and it will give you the strength to start, and then continue on.

What gets you out of bed in the morning? On Sunday evenings, what it is that excites you about Monday morning? What is it that you can't wait to get started on?

A good way to understand this is to dig into the past; that's what works for me. This can be general; the things you loved to do as a kid. It could be anything: maybe exploring, painting, building, jumping — whatever you come up with, the answer is usually in there somewhere.

Finding your thing in this world is super-important and once you have found it, if you have the possibilities and the energy to make it happen (be it small or big, side project or new career), the direction will be clear. Even without being aware of it, every action we take from that moment on will directly or indirectly lead us toward that space of success.

Picking the Right Area

When picking an idea, you should try to keep yourself from investing time in the wrong area. Even though everything is possible, to avoid disappointment, choose an idea based on your personal strengths or your areas of expertise and interest, and you will be willing and able to learn more quickly than had you chosen something outside your scope of interest. Developing something that taps into the skills you already have will help you solve problems that will invariably surface. A completely new business model is possible, and potentially more rewarding, but it will take you longer, that's all.

I don't want to kill any dreams, because this book is supposed to do the opposite; but if you are a creative type and want to become a mathematician, for example, then even with the best intentions in the world you will probably struggle to achieve this dream — and if by chance you do, you probably won't be very good at it.

Knowing your strengths and expertise is of the utmost importance. I recommend you do your best to use them, and then some.

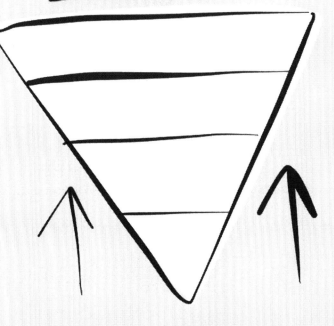

REVERSE

ENGINEERING

Reverse-Engineering Exercise

It can be hard to choose which idea to pursue if you have more than one, so within that realm, it is only wise to start with the ones which will grant us the greatest rewards.

Reverse-engineering is a very useful exercise that will help you think in a different way and will add some clarity when filtering your ideas.

Sometimes it's not the actual *thing* we dream of doing that we are really yearning for, even though we believe it is; usually it's the direct impact that a particular idea or project will have on our lives that really lights us up.

Let me explain myself. For example, if you say you want to launch a magazine about cars, before jumping, the question you need to ask yourself is, W*hy do I want to launch a car magazine?* And then you can add, *because I like cars*, and *I like photography*, and *I like reading*, or *I like writing*, or *because I enjoy talking to people about it when selling ads*. Why? Really ask yourself *why?* This is the first layer; the second layer will be to take one of these answers and dissect it further.

Sticking with this same example, if the answer that resonates most is that you would like to launch a car magazine because you love talking to people about it, because you like cars, and because you like to be flexible with your time, then you may have discovered something. Based on these findings, maybe a car magazine is not the only thing you could do to fulfil those desires. From here, you could start ruminating on what other ideas or businesses you could do that might give you what you really seek.

Instead of thinking that what you want is a magazine, you may realize that what you need to do is something related to people, with flexible working hours, within the car industry. That could translate into something else. Now, with this new brief, any idea we may have within this domain could potentially work. We have now expanded our options. If we decide that a magazine is not what we want to, or can do, we'll be able to do something more in line with our interests, that at the end of the day will give us the same satisfaction and potentially be more profitable.

So remember, it's equally important to consider the outcome you would like the idea or project to have on your life to reverse engineer the project itself.

Look Around for Inspiration- Chasing Ideas

Ideas can come from literally anywhere. They may not necessarily be presented to you in a finished shape; they may be the natural consequence of consuming tons of other ideas, researching, being nosy — until eventually, within no particular time frame, they will appear before you. Don't rush it, but don't stop looking either; they won't become apparent if we are doing something else entirely. At this stage everything goes: books, people, films, dreams.

Pay attention to people whom you admire, but not for what they have done — (as that may not be related to what you want to do) but for how they have done it. For example, biographies are a great source of inspiration to me. Once you have read a few you start understanding the thinking and behavior of the doers in any field. And don't only look on the Internet — magical things happen off the screen too. Listen to podcasts and documentaries, but not passively. Stay awake, stay *on*. Yes, if you are a doer you need to be *on* 24/7. It won't hurt, you will do it naturally. Remember, you *want* to make stuff happen!

Ideas vs. Business Ideas

Look for the idea, and right after it appears, think about how to make money with it. It's important to know that 90% of all great ideas are not necessarily good business ideas. If your next thing does not include seeking profitability, that's ok, but if it does, the question you need to ask yourself is, how the hell are you going to make money with it?

Whether it is B2B, B2C, B2B2C, or an e-commerce store, each will have its own target customers and value configurations, and your capacity to meet the requirements will define your success rate. So don't skip over any of these options without pre-analysis and reflection on your idea. Even though it's likely that your business model will change along the way, it is important to collect information about revenue models, including the very basic ones. There is no need to be a finance person, just do the simple math; it will probably not be accurate at this point but it doesn't matter, you don't want this to stop you from doing it, and anyway at least you won't be starting off in the red.

Bad Ideas Are Good Ideas

"Those who are crazy enough to think they can change the world usually do."

— Steve Jobs

If you already have your idea and everybody tells you it's a bad idea, then stop right there — that's great news! The idea is probably a really good one. If they say it's crazy, it is probably courageous or innovative; if they say you shouldn't do it, and you'll never make it, then you definitely *should* go ahead and do it. You will find innovative ways to deal with problems along the way.

If everybody thinks it's a great idea, then you're probably not doing anything overly innovative, and that's fine, but just be aware of it. Don't let yourself get discouraged by people telling you your idea is bad. Just hear them out and then do whatever you want — -they will be helping you either way.

The Day-After Test

When we start playing with ideas it is very common to get overly excited and experience a high of adrenaline and dopamine. This is that feeling of *Yes, this is it!* And because we want to decide on what we want to do more than anything else, and do it quickly, we often grab the first idea we have and decide it's the one. This will seem like the best idea at the time, especially if you are brainstorming with someone else and especially if that conversation is happening in a bar with a glass (or two) of wine.

The day-after test is a really good one. It's simple: when this happens, the best thing to do is go to bed and re-evaluate your idea the next day — (if you still remember it). You may find that for some reason it doesn't sound quite as enthralling as it did the night before. but perhaps it still does. If so, and though it might be a less euphoric *yes*, you need to keep working on it and keep on sleeping on it. If, after a while, it is still alive, you have probably found something. If not, keep looking.

Analysis Paralysis

Enough is enough, let's start doing!

In this game, if you think too much, you lose. It's show-time now. Pick one idea and go ahead with it. You can change your mind later, and anyways it will most likely change on its own accord somewhere down the line.

Now you need a plan and you must start dividing your tasks and coming up with a little bit of a strategy, a little methodology around achieving your goal. But remember this, you need to be crazy enough to marry your idea, but also (and at the same time) be ready to cheat on it if you find better things along the way.

Being in love with another person gives you a natural high that makes you do amazing things, and so does falling in love with an idea. The difference here though is that you need to fall head over heels with your concept but be ready to leave it at the altar when better things come along as a consequence of the process. Blind monogamy has no place in the incubation of ideas!

Let's not forget that you shouldn't be focusing too hard on the things you want to do. You need to understand what they are going to bring to your life. This way, if things change (and they will) you don't need to feel bad about changing the original plan, as long as you know that your new direction is edging you toward the same sort of benefits you seek. If the new route is taking you to a totally different destination, you should stop and reconsider whether you just need to stop and decide whether it's really what you want to do. It will be your call.

In the words of the late, great Elvis Presley: "a little less conversation, a little more action, please".

CHAPTER 5

Starting and Enduring

This chapter is going to talk about how to get going and how to endure through the sure to be ups and downs that come your way.

Don't Start With an Exit in Mind

If the idea of an exit is what motivates you before you even start, I would be really careful. At the beginning, all you will be doing, or mostly be doing, is building stuff up from scratch, in order to grow and move forward. However, if you start thinking *when is this going to end?* you need to ask yourself why. If you are an angel investor that's fine; actually, it is precisely what you should be looking for — speedy returns. But if you aren't, and the exit plan is the only thing that moves you, you will probably find it very difficult when tough times hit. In this case, I would suggest you stay where you are because if you don't sell out, you will be stuck with something you always wanted to get rid of in the first place. Not a good situation.

Sailing Toward Your Goal

Start sailing with a goal in mind, but don't fight the wind. You can't beat it as it will just throw you sideways, but you can certainly work with it and allow it to take you to places you hadn't planned on visiting. Eventually you will reach your chartered destination, just maybe not by following the same coordinates you anticipated at the start.

Go with the side winds, never in a straight line. You must be able to adapt. Sometimes, you will have to drift astray, but as long as you can see your objective, even though it may be far distant at this point, you're on the right track. As long as you are moving toward it, you're fine. You must keep sailing diagonally.

Things do take time. Often good things take longer than we'd like, and can sometimes take an entire lifetime, but sometimes it's less. None of this matters though, as long as you are doing your thing.

Share Your Idea With Others

Alright, so now you have a defined idea. Don't be too precious with it; remember, it's not the idea, but the *execution* of the idea that is important. In order to discover new things, you must first be willing to share. Not everybody is waiting to steal your grand and unique idea. And if they do steal it, well at least then you know you're capable of coming up with ideas worth stealing; and if you yourself didn't steal it from someone else in the first place, you'll be able to sleep at night knowing there are more ideas where that one came from.

No ideas are entirely new or completely original; everything has been pretty much already been done, but what will always draw crowds are interactions and the evolution of preexisting ideas.

It's difficult enough for an idea to see the light of day, so imagine how impossible it would be if it never even leaves the drawer in the first place. Get out there for goodness sake and start sharing!

This is the time to get out there and talk. The power of sharing your ideas with other people is incalculable, even if you're talking to people that are not obviously related in any way to your concept. If your idea sits within the sports world you don't necessarily have to talk to people who are part of that universe, even though that will of course give you some really good insights. Try sharing with a diverse cross-section of people; explain what you want to create, or what you are already doing — that triggers, in the majority of people, a willingness to help.

I have recently started sharing a new idea I have with someone. I told them what I was working on and I received an enormous amount of unexpected and very useful help. I hadn't asked for it, but I guess I must have talked about it in a way that made them feel like, *How I can help this guy?* This idea may have been resonating in their heads so that when they were at work, at home, travelling or talking to other people, they naturally asked for relevant information, or anything that could help me. It was authentically kind and very helpful to receive all this goodwill.

The power of sharing ideas has unimaginable outcomes; that is why it always makes me laugh when people are sharing their projects, especially if it's their first time, and before they reveal their big idea, they ask you to sign an NDA (non-disclosure agreement). But the *ideas* themselves belong to nobody. It's all in the execution — that's what makes or breaks an idea. The same concept executed by three different people will create three different outcomes. Don't be afraid of sharing your ideas with others.

AIM FOR
MOVE
MENT

Aim for Movement, Not Perfection

In the search for the perfect way, best-case scenario and ideal timing, we spend our lives postponing the most important tasks. Let's crack on with it and find those answers along the path.

I believe in movement more than I believe in planning. You will adjust and adjust again; rinse and repeat. And above all, learn to move forward because perfection will actually never arrive. It is in the *seeking* of perfection that we find new ways to do things better every day. We are constantly looking for the perfect way to do something. In this process we find greatness, but never perfection. So go ahead and look for it, but don't get frustrated when you can't find it. You will naturally continue to be better than you were the previous day. And if for whatever reason you think you have achieved something perfect, that will be the day you stop learning.

Forget about perfection; aim for movement *towards* perfection. This improvement is the thing we really crave underneath it all.

I believe in small and continuous achievements. This is how we should embark on our journey, taking it step by step. One day, you'll look back and realize that these small milestones, small adventures and imperfections are what made your journey meaningful. At some point you'll realize that you have crossed an ocean, or at least reached the middle, and it's not worth going back because half the journey has already been logged.

Movement is life, so keep moving. You can't tread water forever because if you stay still for too long, eventually you will drown; its natural law. Get out there and confront the challenges. Overcome them the best way you can and that will suffice. Those who stay in the false security of their confines will be dead before they know it, or even worse, walking dead.

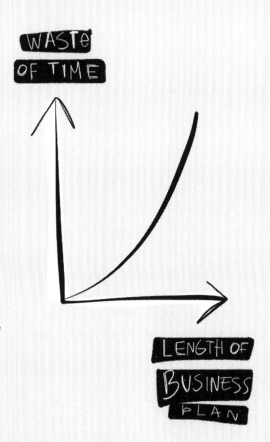

Forget About Fancy Business Plans

A business plan is not necessarily the first step. In fact, business plans are best written after the fact. After what? After you actually know what you are doing. The true and real reaction to your idea comes from the market after you have actually started. Business plans are simply intentions; nothing more, nothing less. They are useful for organizing your thoughts and that's about it. If you're looking for investment opportunities, you *will* have to craft an impressive business plan but apart from that, what matters most are the people behind your plan, their stamina and their will to do something great.

Do not fear the business plan. Don't hide behind it and don't spend too much valuable time on it because it is really just a written intention and a potential roadmap of your journey.

I am not against creating a business plan. I'm just suggesting that you not waste too much mental energy on it. By all means, create one for yourself, it certainly helps to think clearly about some important aspects that, due to excitement or lack of experience you may have overlooked; but those things will come up sooner or later regardless, and you will have to deal with them when they do.

So, instead of just piling up documents and files, let's learn to *do* and deal with these things by actually doing them. On paper we can appear to have it all figured out, but in reality, nothing's been done yet. Let's learn to leave the comfortable bubble surrounding our laptops. Don't let the crafting of a business plan stop you from starting the *work*. Do-It-Yourself, like when you go to the local DIY store - how much in, how much out, how much left, does it work or not?

Don't worry if you don't have the technical and academic aptitude you think you need to create a good business plan. Most people get nervous and frustrated and they tend to stop or delay the process of starting. This is because they think that the first and most important thing to do is make a business plan and as they cannot yet make it, they stop before they begin.

Let me tell you something, anybody can write a business plan; just google it and you'll find a variety of templates to choose from. All you have to do is just sit, apply a bit of common sense and voila - you have a business plan. But having an idea and going for it is *not* what everybody does. *That* is what you have and *that* is what makes you special; taking an idea that lives in your head and making it real. That is what makes you a doer.

Create a Visual: Put It on the Table and Start a Conversation

Visualization has extraordinary powers. We all know most athletes and top performers practice visualization as part of their pre-competition preparation. They imagine and see themselves winning, going faster, going farther. And they do it over and over again. When you see something, half the job has been done. It's incredible how we can trick our brains. All of a sudden it feels real, and all the problems we think we need to deal with in order to make it happen are forgotten, and most importantly, when we share it, we are all talking about the same thing, no confusion.

We can explain things, concepts and/or ideas using our words, but when we put all those words into an image, *Boom!* And immediately everybody is on the same page; you have significantly reduced the possibility of misinterpretation of the same concept and all of a sudden, the *thing* is there and everybody is talking about the same *thing.* Once you have that in the form of a visual aid (illustration or prototype), you start working in a different dimension, one which is more productive, more realistic, more believable.

It may not be a professional illustration or image, it doesn't necessarily need to be a 3D model; it could be a simple hand-drawing, of an object or concept. The media you choose doesn't matter but do make an image of it. Use it for yourself and when talking to others.

Day after day, we can get confused. Life itself throws us into situations that we didn't see coming, so it is important to have our goals and destinations clearly in front of us, whatever they may be. Simply create an image of your goal and look at it every day.

KEEP CALM AND JUST TELL ME

Don't Sell, Just Tell

When starting something new, a whiff of desperation sometimes emanates from our anxiety. Stop yourself from doing that, please — it shows. And don't try too hard — that shows too. It's not attractive, and it is rather embarrassing. Nobody wants to be sold anything. You or your new venture may be really great and in most cases, you're probably proficient at putting forward your concept, but if you're not great at selling it, don't let it get to you. The fact is that everybody is selling something all the time. The difference is in the *how*.

So, if you don't like selling or you think you're not really good at it, I have some good news for you; there's no need to sell. Just tell people what you're up to, what your challenges are, what you're trying to do — and people will listen. This way, if they think they can benefit, or they can help you, they will do it of their own volition; if not, nothing happens. All good. At least that person will still think highly of you, because of your passion and commitment to your project and because you are *doing* it. And most importantly, they will respect you because you didn't try to sell them anything.

People see through facades; they read your body language, they feel your passion (or lack of it) and hear the intensity in your voice. The best thing is to tell them what you are up to, and good things will come back to you.

Where Do I Start?

It's easy to get confused and overly excited at the beginning, but we need to be sure that the energy and resources are being directed to the best possible places. Even though I said it doesn't matter where you start, as long as you start, it is also true that a little bit of common sense doesn't hurt either.

Naturally, we tend to avoid the most difficult tasks involved in making our dreams come to life. We usually find ourselves doing less relevant things and we waste time and vital energy in places where they will have no real impact on the process, growth and success of our venture. For example, sometimes we begin by choosing the furniture; we buy fancy computers, stationery, office equipment, tech gadgets and so on. We start spending before we start making any money. It's important to have a comfortable and maybe even a cool working space but it's not an absolute necessity. You essentially just need a nice space furnished with the basics: a simple table, a comfy chair, a screen, white walls and voilà! That's it. That should suffice. The rest will come, but first you need to focus on more important tasks.

A good way of figuring out what to do next is to imagine that you have a 'go-live' deadline in 10 days from today. What would you prioritize or do first in that time frame? You'll soon understand that going out shopping for a new outfit or buying a fancy office chair is totally irrelevant at this point, and when the obvious steps appear in front of you, you'll know. Usually the basic stuff is where you should focus first. There will be time later for nice office furniture and fancy computers.

The following exercise will give you a preliminary list of things we must do first:

If your idea is to launch a product and if you were me, you would probably start thinking about the ad campaigning, the cool designs, the e-commerce, marketing strategy and so on, but actually the first and only thing you need to do, would be to focus on the product and acquire some inventory. Otherwise, what are you going to sell? We need to start from the inside-out. You would need a supplier that could produce your product, in a particular design. So find a supplier, and get the designs done.

After doing the most important tasks, you can carry on with the rest.

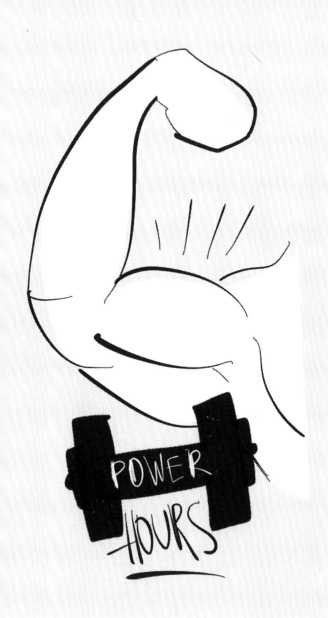

Identifying the Power Hours of Your Day

Understand how your body works and which hours of the day you perform at your best. It should not be difficult to find out. For me and for the majority of us, it is mid-morning, before lunch. Once you have found your own power hours, you can organize your long list of tasks around those times.

The secret is to know when you have more energy, motivation, and focus. Basically when you can produce more, better and quicker. Remember that time is your most important asset. Once you have found your power hours, do all the important tasks during those hours. And you can leave all other duties, the things that require less brain power or are not as critical to your objective, to your less productive hours. They will still get done, but it won't matter so much how alert or focused you are while you're doing them. Keep this in mind and schedule mental breaks for the part of the day when your attention span is at its shortest.

There is also a study that says that we tend to think more creatively when we are tired. This doesn't apply in my case because when I'm tired, I'm useless and I just want to sleep, but if you are like the majority of the sample population, then when you're tired, fatigue and drowsiness will free up nonlinear thinking and will help you in finding new and creative solutions to existing problems.

The bottom line here is to understand how you work your best. Forget about common ways and hours of working and create your own schedule based on your biological clock. You will do much better this way.

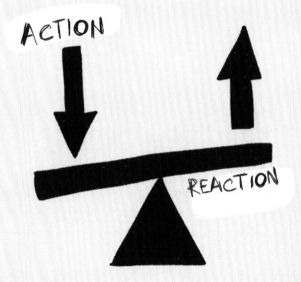

Identify the Small, Achievable Chunks

Newton's Third Law says that "For every action, there is an equal and opposite reaction".

We are not going anywhere if we are not doing anything. The start is more important than the planning. Let's understand that by using an example. If we look up at the top of a long staircase from down below, before we even start climbing the steps the task can appear overwhelming and unachievable. To avoid being overwhelmed and paralyzed, focus on the first step only. Don't think about or put your energy anywhere else, especially as you continue your climb. Focus solely on each next step and not only will you do it better but you will enjoy it more. Once you are there you will have a better, more realistic perspective for the following step, and so on.

Cut the complex elements down into smaller and more easily achievable tasks to mitigate the seeds of fear. Don't look at the whole thing all at once because after fear comes paralysis... action will compound.

Give, Give, Give

Business and real life are not completely separate from each other. In your business or venture, as in life, you will have to help others before you expect anything back in return. This help can take any form. You can offer information, product or troubleshooting services. Help others solve their small problems and they will help you solve your bigger problems. Help them get closer to their goals and desires and eventually, they will come back to you. It is a law of nature. You give, and you receive. Simple and powerful. This step is not as difficult as it sounds. When you're helping others, you realize that apart from attaining material goals, you also feel happier and more satisfied. What goes around comes around.

Validate Your Idea:
Work for Free

Work for *free?!* Bear with me here. In my experience, it's not useful to ask people whether they will use your product or services before developing them. You can do this when you have developed a product and you have something that your customers can try. But even so, in the early stages, I wouldn't recommend you spend a lot of energy, time and money on asking around.

However, I do believe in small tests (like the so-called MVP: minimum viable product) where you create something and put it in front of potential buyers or clients, and let them play, let them talk. *That* is where the real and valuable information will come from, and not before. That is your investment. Let them take it home if it's a product, and if it's a service, offer it for free. This is how you can keep adjusting the offer and understand how to do better. This isn't breaking news, but when you're offering a service, the best thing is to do it for free and build trust; because as you probably know by now, trust, especially in services, is the most valuable currency.

Working for free at the beginning is a great investment.

Let me share with you an example from my life. When I started my previous digital agency, we created, designed and built 14 apps for free in the early stages. We did it for nobody. We just thought about possible sectors and businesses that might need our services and could benefit from our apps. We built the apps proactively. Once ready, we called different people from those sectors and showed them our products. They were very impressed with our work, even though they didn't buy anything. Was it charity? *No.* It was actually a move that helped us build a relationship of trust with our potential customers. It also helped us spread the word about our services.

At the time, we didn't have a specific direction so we opted to channel our energy into *doing* stuff. Our goal was to build something concrete even though we were aware of the possibility of failure. But we did it anyway because this step was crucial to determining our direction and the needs of our market. Simply put: in order to receive, you first need to give.

Do something. Put it on the table and start a conversation.

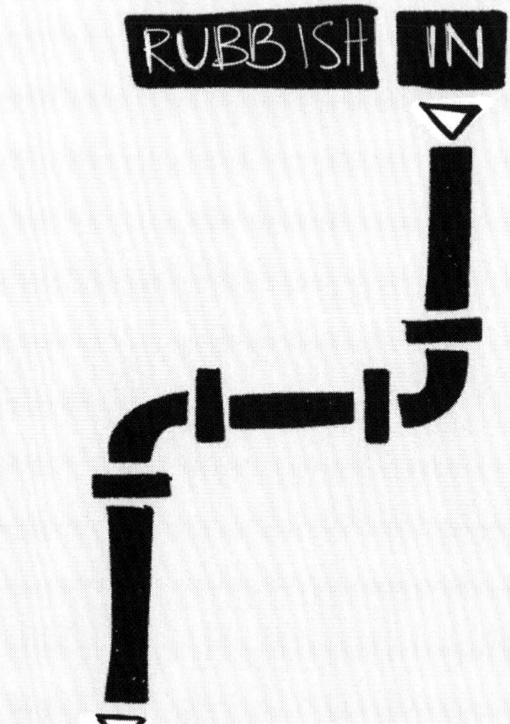
RUBBISH IN
RUBBISH OUT

You are What You Eat

Okay, now you need to focus. Prior to this, you were entertaining an idea, going walkabout, and it was all good. But now you need to stop, and get focused.

Make sure that everything you do, everything you read, the people you talk to and listen to, make sure it's all good stuff. Make sure it's relevant, somewhat connected, or can be useful. If you want to be a doer, you need to value your time like no one else; time is scarce, so use it thoughtfully and invest it properly.

Just as the food you eat is digested to create fuel and the building blocks of your body, everything that goes into your head becomes part of who you are and how you think. As an adult, you can choose to filter what you absorb mentally, so choose quality. I'm not saying you need to ingest uniform input; on the contrary, you can, and probably should, consume a wide range of content, as long as it's high quality and viewed with the right lens.

That's how you'll start connecting the dots. Never lower your guard because the minute you do, you'll find yourself mindlessly consuming information that you haven't consciously chosen, and that can lead to one of the ultimate sins of a doer - mental masturbation. And I hate to break it to you, but watching a tv series isn't going to do you any favors either. Have you ever considered how much time you waste watching tv? Imagine what you could have done with that time instead to move your ideas forward.

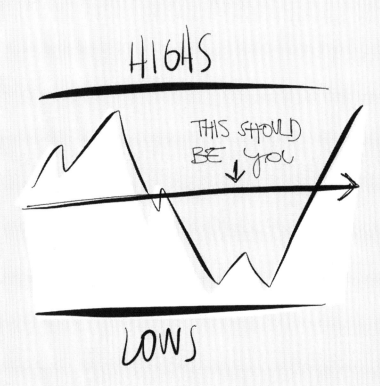

Avoid Low Lows and High Highs

In the process of building something new or starting up, it's totally normal to go through moments when you're feeling really high and on some other days, really low. You might not see the light at the end of the tunnel all the time but trust me, this is all very normal, and it also depends on the type of person you are. Stay cool.

There's a very fine line dividing the whole thing and dictating how we feel. Some days we are gods and goddesses, and other times we feel amongst the lowest on the food chain. Shifting just 1 millimeter to either side can change absolutely everything, even though we have barely moved in reality, and are still in the same place.

The best thing to do is to ignore all of this, and keep moving forward. Look ahead and a touch higher, step by step; if we don't, we may have a false illusion and quit too early or believe that we've already made it before we event start.

Feet on the ground, head to the sky.

Learning to Love Rejection

You're starting something new and you need to adjust to a new world. Fall in love with rejection because it's not the outright rejection that is important, it's the underlying reason for that rejection that we should value and therefore embrace. Whatever you are looking for, whether it's the next step, the next answer, or any other thing, the answer lies within the reason for that rejection.

Look for the *No;* that's where the next *Yes* is. This is priceless feedback. Feedback is data. Data is knowledge. Feedback will bring you closer to your goal, and much faster. There's no such a thing as negative or positive feedback; I believe there is expected and unexpected feedback. What you want is the unexpected feedback: that which you do not already know.

Don't remain on the surface after rejection, expose yourself, go deeper. *No* is the answer? Great, but why? Or why not? If *this* is not the way, which direction would be better?

The general rule of thumb is, after asking *Why?* at least three times, you will start to uncover something valuable. That's where the meat is. And don't forget to celebrate afterward.

Many years ago, I had a design firm, and every time we lost business, or received a rejection of some sort from a client, instead of worrying or feeling sad, we would go out to the most expensive café or bar in town and have lunch or dinner to celebrate. At the beginning it felt unnatural and contrived, but I soon got used to it, and even began to enjoy it. Believe me, something greater invariably arrived on the heels of each rejection. So don't forget to celebrate rejection, and of course, victories too.

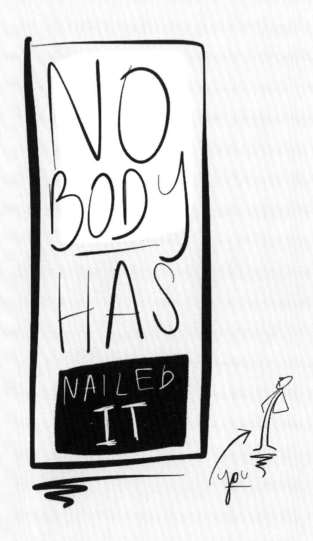

Nobody Has Actually *Nailed It*, No Matter What They Say

It's very common at the beginning of our road, when you are still just a young business, to observe people or companies that are doing great, and self-reflect on your own achievements, or lack of thereof. First of all, and as I've said before, remember that everybody is selling something; so in a world of highly successful people and companies, it's rather easy to become demoralized, especially when social media, is incessantly showing you how great everything is going for *everyone* but you.

But guess what? It's just not true. Everybody is fighting something and struggling with one thing or another — they just choose not to put all of it on display. You rarely get to see the dark sides of people's lives. And it's not even about the struggle, it's the way you deal with it. And thinking in a reactive way will only make you lose confidence in yourself; it will make you feel tired and like quitting before you've even begun.

It's easy to think that everybody else has it easier than us, but that self-pity won't get you anywhere; in fact, if you dig deeper, many of those who appear to display greatness, are actually struggling or have struggled. It is, in part, what has made them stronger and shaped their character or businesses into what that they needed to be in order to succeed.

So, it's all well and good to look at what other people are up to, but never compare yourself to them. Learning from others - yes. Comparing yourself with others - no. Compare and compete with you and only you.

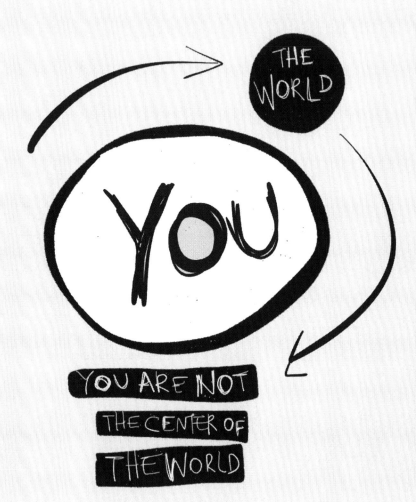

You Are Not The Center of The World

When you're just starting up, and later on too, you want everything *now*. You call hundreds of people and send hundreds of emails and you expect people to respond right away. Relax. Breathe. This just isn't how things work. You have to be patient. Just because someone didn't reply immediately doesn't mean they never will, or that your idea or project is a dud bound to fail, or that they don't like you. It means that they're simply doing something more important for *them* at that particular time. Remain calm. The seed is planted. Move on and rest assured that it will eventually grow.

When you need a response from someone, don't panic. People aren't thinking about you all the time; they're too busy thinking about themselves. Naturally, their world doesn't revolve around you. Reach out to them and if they give you an answer, whether it's positive or negative, it's completely fine. And if they don't respond at all, that's ok too. But you need to keep going and understand that it's a *process*.

To really grasp this, imagine a long road ahead of you and as you walk, you throw seeds on both sides. Many of those seeds won't sprout at all, but eventually, some will become amazing trees. Some seeds will take longer than others to germinate and some will sprout and grow quickly. Never give up during your first steps. You must keep waiting for your seeds to grow, and this process requires patience and determination. You have to keep going about your business because other people are busy minding their own. Most of them, perhaps unfortunately, live extremely fast lives and tend to forget pretty much everything that isn't urgent. They'll call you when they need you.

Just Say *Yes*. You'll Figure Out the Rest, Later

Just say *yes*. You can figure everything out later. This isn't lying, it just means you're ambitious and courageous. Nobody is born knowing. There are a lot of very capable people out there, and for many different reasons either they didn't achieve their full potential or their ideas or projects never become known. It's a real pity for them and for humanity.

From scientists to artists, athletes to visionary entrepreneurs; for some reason or another they lack the confidence and courage to really go out there and shine. Its blaringly obvious to those from the outside looking in but sadly they don't even see it and they simply choose not to play the game. Life isn't fair. I know people like this, and I'm sure you do too. I've seen it too many times to count. The world is full of less-than-capable people making big decisions that impact the lives of the masses. And so many great humans remain in the shadows; talented people who feel the need to obey and bow to others not necessarily smarter than they are even when they do not agree with the direction they are following.

So, what's the difference between these two types of people? IQ? Capability? Talent? None of the above. The only difference is that some dare to do what others won't. They have confidence and courage. It's the natural chain of things. Do, or be done to. Eat, or be eaten.

With this in mind, the next time you face a challenge, you will undoubtedly rise to it and say *Yes!* You can, and you *will* figure out the rest, later. Keep this concept in mind because when you are starting something new, there is no room for self-doubt.

BE FRUGAL

Always Be Frugal

Be careful and be frugal. Be mindful of your time, money and the opportunity costs. Find the right balance and be ready to gamble it all. But also know that the longer the rope and the bigger the time frame you give yourself, the more tranquility and clarity you will have to work with. This is basically what freedom is.

What is most important to you? Don't try to tell me that fancy dinners and expensive clothing take precedent over your dreams — of course they don't. And working within that frugal mind-frame, it's easy to keep your expenses low for a truly great cause, and your main objective: Success.

Using Aids to Keep Going

You have to stay strong throughout your journey. The beginning is tough. Building something from scratch is never easy. There will be rough times, but you must never give up. Just do *whatever* is necessary. Trick your brain to prevent it from taking you to dark places. I remember my early days when I first moved to London, while I was still trying to learn English. I used to look at people on the train, especially the ones that didn't look particularly intelligent — and *they* were all speaking English! I used to say to myself, *Ok, if they can, I can.* Use anything that can help you believe in yourself and your dream. As silly as it may seem, if it works, keep doing it.

Another good tactic is to observe people you like and admire. If there is someone who has achieved things that you respect and would like to emanate, it's important to understand how they did it. It's also important to look at other kinds of people too, people you can't really relate to, or even those you may be less than fond of. This is valuable because if they are actually doing stuff and getting recognized for it, regardless of what it is they do, or who they are, what *is* it they are doing that you're not? What risks do they take that you're not taking? Check them out and learn from them.

Lean on whatever you need to help you endure. Just like Diane Nyad, the long-distance swimmer who claimed that she managed to swim from Cuba to Florida, a distance of about 110 miles (180 km) because of a deep belief in perseverance — and some really good songs. She said that singing a playlist to herself over and over again, anchored by John Lennon's "Imagine" played more than 100 times, helped tremendously. So, there you go.

Stay Close to Your Product or Service

Get your hands dirty and do the work yourself. Nobody will do it for you, or as good as you can. Of course, it's equally true that delegating is an art and that's how you grow, (in my experience). Although delegating *is* important, it is equally important that you yourself are capable of doing integral things for your project, especially at the very beginning. It's easier at this point because at least you are starting small. If you do it your way, you are more likely to be resourceful and that is to your advantage. However, as you grow you should make that the norm. By doing so, you will develop an in-depth knowledge of your product or service which is vital, and you will be able to walk the walk and talk the talk — and that can't be bought.

When things go well and your venture is growing, you will be required to delegate, but again, remember things also change. When change happens, you need to be able to shrink the whole operation to its minimum expression — meaning, *you* — and still be able to run it. If you don't know how to do that, you could be in real trouble. But if you do, you will always be able to survive when hard times come knocking.

Stay close to the core of your project, and even though you certainly won't have to downscale on a regular basis, make sure you're at least close enough to the core that you can easily learn *how* to run it alone if need be. This is the best way to hedge your bets and protect your business from future turbulence.

If you are in the business of repairing cars and your company grows, you go from repairing two cars to repairing fifty. At this point, you're more likely to stop working on them yourself and hire staff to do it for you, and that's natural, but make sure you never forget how to fix a car, and that you frequently immerse yourself in the garage environment. If for any reason the business goes belly-up, and you find yourself with just one car to repair, you should be able to do a good job of fixing it yourself, and have some food on the table at the end of the day.

It's not always easy to find the balance between delegating jobs that could be done satisfactorily by others, and at the same time staying close to the core of your business, but you should ensure that you never lose sight of those central workings. Failure to do so could leave you vulnerable in the future.

If You're Going to Fail, Fail Better

I met with a man once who had a lot of business experience, and who later became a partner on a particular venture I created. At our first meeting he asked me how many times I had been broke, or how many times I had failed in my professional life. I candidly replied that I had failed *many* times; to which he said, "Good, then let's talk business." For him, more than anything else, a potential partner had to have had those experiences; had to have fallen down and gotten up again: a person who understood that failure is an integral part of the process of doing or building anything. He also told me that a few more times would have been even better!

So-called failures are the turning points in our lives, and are where the real learning happens; the rest are words easily blown in the wind.

I must confess that I have a particular attraction to doing new things and failing at them, because those are the moments when I feel most alive. They are the moments, the dots that we will later connect, which will grant us great future achievements. Failures are the scaffolding on which we build who we are and what we do.

In the end, the hard times are the most memorable times of all. They shouldn't be teaching perfection in schools, they should be teaching bravery and resilience and celebrating failure. But having said that, maybe it's hard to explain to a 9-year-old that it's great to do everything wrong…

So, fail, fail again, fail better, then watch the success happen.

And as a bonus, making mistakes actually makes us more likeable, due to something called the Pratfall Effect. Those who never make mistakes are perceived as less likeable than those who do make them. Perfection creates distance, based on an unattractive air of invincibility. So if we keep failing forward, we win in the end.

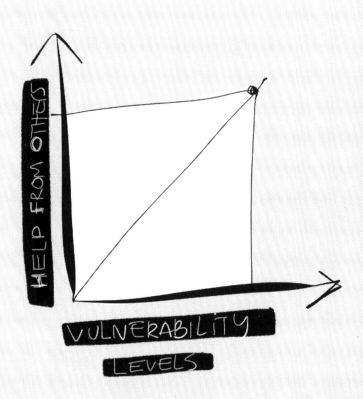

You Are Vulnerable, and That's Your Strength

We all are vulnerable to some degree but at this early stage, you are likely to be at your most vulnerable. But contrary to popular belief, vulnerability is not a weakness and can be used in your favor. It pays to be vulnerable because honesty is what makes people feel like helping us, and in a world of fake news and deceptive social media, it also gives us the uncommon allure of being *real*.

Tell your true story. You don't need to pretend to be anything or anyone else. Just be humble, and make sure that it's real. A little bit of creative license and storytelling is fine and to be expected, but people admire most those who stand honestly for what they believe in and who have the courage to try new things. If you are one of those brave souls then don't hide it because there is pride in it. If someone wants to help you, don't see it as pity. Accept support where it is offered — we may be doers but we still need all the assistance we can get.

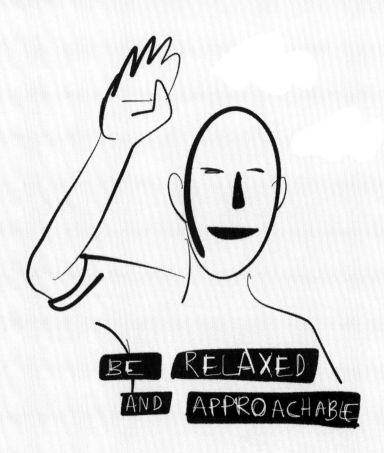

Be Relaxed and Approachable

You don't need to be boring if you want to be taken seriously. Of course you need to be laser-focused about achieving whatever it is you're striving for, but at the same time you don't need to be stiff or mundane in order to do it properly, or to come across as being good at something. We are human. We are social animals. We thrive on interaction, and even though these days we may be doing so less directly, physical and social interactions (analogue or digital) are still very important, if not more so. When you do interact with others, make sure you are as human and present as you can be.

If it feels right, it *is* right. Simple and powerful, and definitely more fun.

It Pays Off to Be Honest

As obvious as this may sound, in business as in real life, being honest is good business. Especially in today's economic sector, where everything is very confusing and values in business are not above suspicion. We hear, now more than ever before, of the tyranny and barbarities that some companies and powerful individuals call normal business practices. Unfortunately, deceit is their malignant currency and people have come to accept lies as the norm. But that's exactly why being different, being honest, is not only the right thing to do, but It's also good business — and as a bonus, it's convenient for you.

Since you are currently in the starting phase, get off on the right foot and decide to be honest, because it has high value in today's market. It doesn't matter what you do, honesty will always be the best policy.

In order to get something in return, every business is trying to sell you something, or pretend something, or show something; and in the process, hiding the less glamorous side of things. Everybody claims to be a market leader. There's a glitch though. How can *everybody* claim to be top dog? It's just not possible, and credibility is going down the tubes in today's era. In this context, honesty has become a tangible asset in the modern marketplace. And truth be told, it's far less crowded up here.

Do the right thing. Simple.

STAY

KNOWLEDGEABLE

Stay Knowledgeable at All Times

As you forge ahead, a key element at this stage and beyond is to not become complacent. Make sure you are learning new things every day — and you will no doubt be *forced* to learn new things every day in the pursuit of your venture. But this is the key because whatever you do, you will never know enough. Fact.

Many people find the idea of being an eternal student, depressing. If you're in this camp, you might want to consider opening up your mind. Educating yourself isn't just memorizing books for an exam. Education can be as easy as watching a documentary or reading a good book on a fascinating topic. Have you changed your mind yet? You just need to stay curious about your subjects of interest. Always assume that you don't know everything yet, keep asking questions — and Google everything.

Don't stay trapped in the crystal cage that we tend to build around ourselves after doing an activity for quite some time. It may be transparent, but a cage is a cage. There is so much out there to learn, and knowledge will always be power. The difference today is that information is at everybody's fingertips; you're only a click away from new knowledge. You can learn pretty much anything about everything. Soft skills come with experience and real interaction, but all other knowledge is transferable, and it's all out there waiting for you.

Stay Grounded

Let's assume you are doing great and everything is looking good. Maybe you have already started to make some decent money. Stay cool, stay grounded. Success, especially if it's your first time, can sometimes be tricky and misleading, and can make you do things you will regret in the future. Keep your head in the clouds but your feet on the ground.

Not sure *where* you are going? By all means dream wild dreams but don't be stupid about it. If you want to start the next Facebook, go for it, but know your statistics first. Maybe what you actually want to do is somewhere in-between or even smaller. Whatever it is that you're building, make sure it's what you need, and be careful not to forget your daily achievements. They are the building blocks that create a foundation for whatever comes next. No crazy illusions, and no disillusions either. Dream wild and stay grounded.

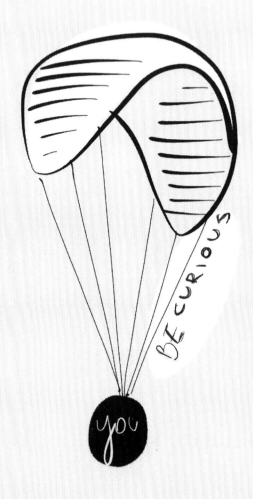

Be Curious — Keep Trying New things — Innovate

Innovation is a word that is sometimes perceived as fluffy, pretentious or scary. How about instead of *innovative* ways, you replace it with *refreshing* ways, or simply *new* ways of doing things.

The best way to innovate, in my experience, is not to look for the innovation itself, but instead to try different tacks, make mistakes, keep doing stuff, and eventually... innovate. That's how we discover unexpected and great things.

The World Music genre was accidentally *invented* by the French-born Spanish artist, Manu Chao. After recording an album while traveling around the world, Chao went back home to Spain to master and release his new record. But while the computer was processing all the audio tracks, it mistakenly deleted the tracks on which the drums had been recorded. Long story short, they released the album anyway, and it was a global success, due to its simplicity and new type of sound.

Micromanagement vs. Nanomanagement

Pretty much every book out there will tell you that micromanaging is a bad thing; that employees hate it, that it keeps people from innovating and makes you a bad leader. I agree that it can have a negative impact on your subordinates, for sure, but this is not a corporate book, it's a book for doers. Doers love what they do, and that passion translates into everything they do. So, my suggestion is, don't bother micromanaging — nanomanage instead. Stay close to *every* aspect of your venture because nobody will care about it the way you do; I repeat, *NOBODY*. Never detach from what made it work in the first place: *You*. Nanomanagement does not mean watching over every employee or service provider's shoulder - rather, it means remaining close to your project in such a way that you know everything that is happening without interfering in the least bit. It is certainly an art rather than a science but one worth becoming an expert at.

Don't Worry, Everything Will Change

The only constant thing in life is change. Be like a Boy Scout and be prepared for absolutely everything. You are a living organism, your business partners (if you have any) are living organisms, the market is a living organism in its own way, as are your surroundings — and your users too, of course, so stay flexible and ready for a change. Embrace the constant movement.

If we embody this thinking, we'll be better prepared to spot opportunities and adapt, strive and survive. People come and go, it's all part of the game; no drama, just life and business. Ideas come and go, companies come and go, understand that everything is made out of clay and nothing will last forever.

Abandon the idea of foreverness. Everything you create has an expiry date, so take the sting out of it at the outset and be conscious that it will come to an end at some point. Enjoy it now for what it is; it may or may not last a long time, who knows, ideas are not set in stone. This approach will free you up and let you enjoy life. And whatever you are doing, as a consequence, you'll do better.

So embrace finitude; it only allows more new chapters to come. And it's a good thing they do because in today's day and age the old world is irrelevant in certain respects. The concept of getting a job and plugging away at it Monday to Friday until the day you die (or retire first, if you're lucky) is over. Thank goodness, what a drag that was!

Whatever you dream of doing or are already doing, it won't last forever. Constant change is evolution and things will last however long they are meant to last. Don't let that thought kill you before you start your venture.

And Lastly, Be grateful

I sure am, every day.

I would like to thank you for reading this book. I really hope it has nudged you in the right direction. If it has, my goal has been accomplished and now it's your turn to take the reins. But remember, you can disregard every single thing in this book if you want to, and that's more than fine by me. Because there is only one true way, and that's *your* way. Just keep moving and don't stop. If you make sure you do that, you'll be fine.

So let's stop talking and start getting stuff done. You will soon be relishing one of life's most rewarding feelings. It's ok, you can thank me later.

Go for it, and enjoy the ride.

I really hope this book has inspired you to take action. If so, send me an email at manuelduboe@gmail.com I would love to hear your news.

CONTACT

This Book URL
Enoughtalkjustdo.com

Manuel's E-mail:
manuelduboe@gmail.com
manuelduboe@finallyfinally.com

Manuel's Instagram
@manuelduboe

Finally
Design & Creative communications studio

URL: www.finallyfinally.com
Instagram: @Finallyagency
Facebook: Finally agency

Flyinwig
The Art of Riding

URL: www.flyinwig.com
Instagram: @Flyinwig

Thanks

I would like to thank my wife for her love, support, patience, and unwavering belief in me. I want to thank my kids for providing me with a never-ending source of inspiration and drive. To my dear friend Cat MacLaggan who helped me massively with the editing of this book. And to my parents, who helped me identify my path - especially my mother, a brilliant fellow writer with an endless source of energy. These are the ultimate doers in my life. And to all those doers in all disciplines around the world, who keep on inspiring me – thank you.

About The Author

MANUEL DUBOE practices what he preaches. From his own art exhibitions to writing and publishing books, from heading up design & creative studios in top London agencies to starting his own tech business and other ventures — he has always proved himself to be a true *doer*.

Manuel initially studied Design at the University of Buenos Aires, where he later taught, but his curiosity eventually led him to London to study Business. Now based in Spain where he lives with his wife and two boys he works globally, Manuel is also the founder and Creative Director of Finally, a design and creative consultancy firm that merges creative thinking with business knowledge, bridging the gap between these two apparently different worlds.

You can find Manuel working on many other passion projects too, which include a fine art book profits of which are dedicated to a charity for helping children cope with stress, and also the launch of a brand called Flyinwig, an endeavor within the world of motorcycles which celebrates the art of riding. Flyinwig products are currently being created. He is also a prolific artist in his spare time and can be contacted at manuelduboe@ gmail.com

41425208R00111

Made in the USA
Middletown, DE
06 April 2019